THE POWER OF THE HEART AND THE HANDS OF A "CNA"

Certified Nursing Assistant

"AN ACT OF LOVE"

Pamella D. Gordon

authorHOUSE®

AuthorHouse™ LLC
1663 Liberty Drive
Bloomington, IN 47403
www.authorhouse.com
Phone: 1-800-839-8640

Published by AuthorHouse   08/27/2014

ISBN: 978-1-4969-0762-2 (sc)
ISBN: 978-1-4969-0761-5 (e)

Library of Congress Control Number: 2014915378

On your worst day, an encouraging word, said with humility and a smile, can have great impact on anyone's life for the better, even yours and mine.

In this book, I describe my experience as a certified nursing assistant (CNA). I faced many challenges during my initial years in the field, but because of my love and passion for the people I served, I was able to overcome those challenges and continue to do my job to the best of my ability. My approach is to love people first, then you will love your job. A job is never easy, even if you are self-employed. In order to succeed, you must love what you are called to do or chosen to do. Do it with passion.

INTRODUCTION

My journey as a CNA started in 1997 when I was hired to work in a small nursing home in Wayne.

After a while, I was getting the experience that I needed, but somehow I felt cornered. I needed to spread my wings. I was looking for a challenge. Then I learned that the home would soon be closing; it was only a matter of time.

So during that time, I had one foot out the door. I started working from 5:00 p.m. to 9:00 p.m. For a few months, I also worked some professional jobs, which I had done before. The other CNAs admired my work and said, "I like how you work." It was rewarding just to see the smiles on their faces.

In 1996, my husband and I started attending night school; I met this girl, and we talked a bit. I don't remember how far the conversation went, but she must have gotten my address, because one day, the doorbell rang, and there she was at the front door. She came to tell me all about a six-week course for becoming a certified nursing assistant and gave me the address and phone number. I was so happy, I could not wait. Then I realized she lived just above my street.

I called and found out when the class started. I was still working in the other job, but that was not what I really wanted, so I started this class. I couldn't drive, so I had to use the bus. The teacher told us, "If you are not going to read the book, don't bother to start and waste my time." She told us one of the girls in the class had been there before but could not pass. If you failed the six-week course, you had to start over and pay again.

I had just come from Jamaica a year before. I had to take two buses but I got there every morning on time. I clicked with one of the women in the class; she was a Christian from my country,

Jamaica, and lived outside of town. I don't know how she got there.

One of my relatives was in the class also; she had noticed me talking to this woman.

She said, "That lady who talked to you resembles our aunt."

I said, "Yes, you also see the resemblance?"

That aunt of ours had passed away a long time ago.

The teacher said, "Pick who you want to buddy up with," and the woman who looked like my aunt chose me.

Every week, we were quizzed and had to sit in different seats; the ones the teacher wanted to keep an eye on sat close to her. The night before the final exam, I went to bed around three o'clock; I had stayed up studying because I had to pass. It was a piece of cake. That day, everything was locked in my brain. I don't think anyone wasted any time. I went on my way after I passed; no time for celebrating. I had work to do; we were one happy class, and the teacher was so proud of us.

I didn't stop to see if anyone didn't make it. My son was waiting to pick me up. Now I knew my journey had just begun, so when I came home, I told my nearest friend that I passed; she was amazed. I started looking for a job. I always wanted to venture out on my own to check out the nursing homes. I went to one place, but the people were too busy talking; the next one was dingy, and I got out fast. The third place was better; I filled out an application and got hired on the spot. This was in 1997; my first job as a CNA.

I didn't have a car, so I got a ride from family members or my friend, who worked just around the corner from where I was. We were both on the morning shift. Then, my sister bought a new car, so I got her for a change. I learned to drive and passed on the first test. I was scared to drive by myself, so my friend told me to drive in front and she would drive behind to see if I was doing okay.

She gave me the okay, and I was on my way, making applications in upscale nursing homes. I went to one place, and the woman I spoke to wondered how I got in; people said it was very hard to get in there.

I told her this was not the first time I had applied for a job there; it was in a different department, but I never got an answer. This time, I made the application and was called within a short period of time.

The administrator hired me and said, "Why didn't you apply when you got your license? You would get your school money back."

So I was hired on the five-to-nine shift, while I was still working at the first nursing home. It was so close to my home, I could go home in the evening, eat my dinner, and go back to this work; I had time to take care of myself and arrive before five o'clock. As time went on, the other nursing home was about to close, and I was on my toes, because you know nothing is sure. I did get out before it closed, and it wasn't too long before I saw some of the residents coming over to the second nursing home.

So on my journey as a CNA, I have seen a lot of people who were unable to help themselves. I didn't know where I was going from there, but as time passed, I found it very interesting. In 1997, I was hired as a part-time worker. I was moved to another building but told someone I wanted to work in the first building. I didn't have a clue what it contained or what was awaiting me.

I was hired and sent to that same building where I was orientated. That unit was where the alert and MS residents were. On my orientation, one resident told me I couldn't come behind the curtains, so the CNA told me what I had to do for her. It didn't take too long before I knew she was the bully on the floor; I had to go the extra mile.

Days went on, weeks went on, that was my assignment, and she was on it. One afternoon, a resident was crying and making a lot of noise; from across her room, she shouted, "Shut up, you ugly bastard!"

He shouted back, "Shut your fat mouth!"

She yelled, "Shut up with them two ugly sons you have."

I said to her, "No, that's not nice."

She said, "He's ugly, and his sons are ugly."

Whenever there was a bathroom problem with her, I would say, "Do you prefer a shower? It would be easier."

She was the happiest person alive, and every day she would get a shower because of her situation. I'm telling you, we became friends; she would sit at the nurse's station in the afternoon, just waiting and hoping to see me. Even if you felt sick, as long as you could walk, you know they were waiting for you. So when I had my days off, other people would be assigned to her. They told me she didn't want them taking care of her.

The nurse would have to explain to her, "Pam has a personal day or is on holiday."

Sometimes she would look at an aide and say, "I don't like you."

I remember this lady, Miss Will; every Friday, she would get a shower on my shift. I came in at three o'clock, and she was in her power chair at the door in the lobby, waiting for me. She was approaching eighty years old, and some days I did not feel well, but when I remembered her, I had to show up. I remember on some days, two of us were sent to take care of a resident, and one of the CNAs said she did not want to go in his room. Take it from me; this man was not a piece of cake.

So I said, "Are you ready?"

She went in halfway and came back outside, leaned against the wall, and said, "I can't bear to look in his eyes."

Now we had to move fast; time was of the essence.

I said, "Come, you stay quiet; I'll do the talking," so while he talked, I answered and made it pleasant.

I will never forget this; one afternoon, on the three o'clock shift, I was busy putting linens in the rooms. I saw this CNA come to the floor, but he didn't see me. I now was getting ready to go listen to the report, I saw him return. I called out to him; he looked up and saw me. He said, "Hey, Miss Pam, you are here?"

I said, "Where are you going?"

He said, "I was leaving. I can't get the help when I came here, and that could slow you down."

There was a lot of truth to what he said, but you can't only work with who you want to; you have to find your way around people and give a helping hand any time you can, or else your goose will be cooked.

It's a rough field and a delicate one too. I've seen people working one day but then don't know when they leave. I recommended one of my family members to the field of nursing and she made it, although she's very new in it.

There were times when nurses or CNAs would come on the unit, and you could tell it was their first time. They would let you know because they were scared. Some would come and ask you about the residents before they entered.

So one day, I saw this nurse standing at a resident's door. I said to her, "Is this your first time here?"

She said, "No, I was here before."

I said, "Okay, I was going to see this same person too."

The nurse and I went in, and everything was fine until she used the wrong approach with the resident. Everything broke loose; I was shocked.

The nurse could not help what she said, because she was used to talking to her residents in that way, but on this unit, you couldn't.

One of the residents would call me "Flash Gordon." She said, "You are always a step ahead of me, and she would be telling you all what you have to do."

She shared a room with her friend; the friend asked, "How did she end up getting me?"

The friend said, "She is lucky, because our friend here is not a piece of cake; everyone fights with her until they get her off their assignments, then she ends up with me."

When I got her, she was worried, but I told her it would be different. Too much talking would cause confusion. One thing at a time.

I had two primary assignments: Mr. C and Mr. W. They were both in the same room. Mr. C decided that he had to leave the room because of health conditions, so when he left, he was given to another person. He started complaining that he didn't know he was going to lose me as his primary, so he called the head of nursing and got me back. One day, he was sitting in his chair, ready to go to bed, but the nurse assigned him to another person, just to balance the assignments. He was crying like a baby that this CNA could not put him to bed; he would rather sleep in his chair. They were scared when they saw a new person show up.

It took a couple of years before I could have a senior position on the unit; while I "floated," it was challenging to deal with different types of illnesses. I remember one unit I went to; as soon as you put those residents to bed, they were gone. One night, I was looking for this resident to put her to bed, but I couldn't find her. I took the elevator to the lobby, but she wasn't there. When I came back on the floor, I went back to her room and there she was, sitting in her Merri-Walker, listening to music. That must have been my happiest day on the job.

When I first worked on my unit, I was orientated with another CNA. We went into this resident's room around 4:30; only half an hour was required for her, because supper was at five o'clock. That resident made the CNA look as if she had no clue what she was doing. When we got out, all sixty residents had finished eating and had been dispatched to their floor.

We reported to the supervisor the length of time she kept us in the room, because there were assignments in the dining room for us to do.

One of our special residents was Miss U. She would put her light on just to have someone come by, and she would catch me. Sometimes, she asked for me; I remember one CNA told her, "She's not your aide; why are you calling her all the time?"

I felt so bad for her; I would tell her, "I'm coming."

She wasn't my primary, but the way I worked with all of them, they all seemed like they were my primary. That lady would tell me stuff; I knew she trusted me.

After a meeting at the Residents' Council, they sent a letter about me. When I tried to open it, the nurse snatched it from me, saying, "This is good, Pam."

When I read it, it made my night brighter and my work load lighter. That's the praise you never know you would hear from the residents.

In our final hours in that building, one of the residents, almost the last one admitted to the unit, asked me, "Pam, are you thinking of writing a book?"

I said, "It has crossed my mind several times."

She said, "You should go ahead and write it."

Seven years later, another resident asked me if I was writing a book.

I said, "Definitely, yes, soon."

There were some dynamic and dynamite nurses on that afternoon shift; you would never be alone. I give them a lot of credit, because that's how we survived.

When you talked about a family away from home, you didn't have to worry; these people were concerned about each other. We bonded together.

I can remember like it was yesterday: I sat in the lobby on my break, just passing time on the three o'clock shift. Some of the other workers gave a different opinion, and I said, "If this place goes up, I'll ride with it, and if it comes down, I'll come down with it. I have nowhere else to go."

One of our housekeepers just smiled at me. In a minute, a CNA flashed past us; someone looked outside and saw her get into her car. One of us ran outside and went to talk to her; a couple of people were standing out there. She was talking with the lady, who said that she was leaving. When asked why, her reply was, "It is so hard. I can't take it anymore."

She begged her to stay, saying, "That's not the way to go."

She finally got her back inside, and she is still working to this day. It's amazing how fast people quit. After a while, I was the only one left from my hiring group. They told me I'd be the only one left from the group.

The worst thing that happened was when they cut the part-time days. One of the girls cried and said, "I need the hours."

I said, "I am glad to have a little break."

Finally, they told me they were leaving for a full-time job. A couple of years passed, and only two of us who were left from different groups got the full-time positions.

The other girl came running, laughing, and said, "Pam, we got the full time." It was the very one who almost quit; while she was so happy, I started crying. I don't know why I was crying; I felt like I just got hit with a ton of bricks.

A full-time worker told me, "You are going to have every other weekend off," but that again is a different chapter in my life. We knew it didn't come easy. Another girl who wasn't in my group didn't get it. The reason why it was so hard, the supervisor reminded us all the time about our record keeping; it was the best.

While working on the three o'clock shift, I was floating on a different unit when this lady was visiting a family member. She saw me working and asked, "Are you a full-time worker?"

I said, "No."

"How long have you been here?" she asked. I told her.

"Say what? Why do you work so hard? Do you have a family?"

"Yes."

"You have to get a full-time job to cover your family." She didn't know my family was taken care of on other insurance.

At that time, I was taking care of four girls. Come to think of it, while she was talking, I was in the hallway, working. I understood why she was concerned, but I was taught to respect others. I was there with a smile on my face; I think that's why she kept on talking. My mind was already made up, no matter what.

During that period of time, I got as an assignment a resident who was dying; halfway through it, the person died. I had to take care of the dead person all alone; I was shaken, I was afraid. I didn't know him; I'm telling you, I hated that unit.

I floated there again the following day; they called me and said a resident's family member was missing a piece of jewelry. I was the one who put her to bed; I went there and told the family where I had put it; the resident could not talk.

The family said, "You are not the one who took it."

I was sent back to the floor.

I did not even write a report on it. (Amazing.) The following day, they brought the resident's necklace and put it back where they found it.

I saw someone from that unit and asked, "What happened to the necklace?"

They said, "Someone brought it back."

I believe the family member knew who the thief was.

When I got the letter from my supervisor to get the part-time position, she said, "Make me proud, Pam."

I had to go to another supervisor to get the position; this supervisor did not know the position was vacant, because someone was waiting for it.

Evaluation time came around; she called me in the office and read the report she had. She was very straightforward with what you had to know. She would tell you when to take over, step inside, and hold your position so they knew who was in charge. All the residents in the unit loved me by name. When the residents were interviewed by the supervisor, that's what they told her. I knew it, but to hear it made a lot of difference.

One afternoon, the girls were talking about their second jobs; some were looking for another one. It fascinated me, so I opened my mouth, saying, "You think I would be hired right away?"

They said, "Yes, Pam, try it."

I did not want to know where they were working. I already knew the town, so I took off on my own. I had the interview and was hired to work every other weekend. I chose the third shift, believing it would be easier when it was work; how could it be easier?

So one night, while I was driving to work, I was stopped by the cops. I was near a stop light. He asked for my license; I said, "What for?"

He said, "You were speeding."

I couldn't believe it; they just used to see the car coming in at that time, not going out, because he was looking at me for a while. Anyway, I got to work and saw one of my coworkers going home; she said to me. "Pam, aren't you tired?"

"Of course I'm tired," I said. "I just got caught up in the system."

I really wasn't looking for a second job, but it went on for a while, and I was losing my sleep. This kind of career is a delicate one; you need your sleep as much as possible, for alertness and quick action. I could not think slow, especially on my second shift, where sixty residents were depending on me. It doesn't mean you have that entire amount, but if the call lights come on, you have to answer them with no questions asked. It happened that I wasn't at my regular base for a couple of days, so they sent a floater over there for that period. She saw me when I returned and didn't say much, but sources said she quit, along with her friend who was working there. I never saw that girl again. She ended up working my assignment at that time.

In the early days, while training for CNA, I took a class where we had to go to the nursing home to train; while on the training, I saw for the first time all these various types of diseases. I was finished taking care of a resident, when she pick up her pocket book, waved good-bye to us, and said, "I am leaving for work."

I stood there, looking at her. There was no place for her to go; in a couple of minutes, she returned, with a smile on her face.

There was an episode when I was floating from unit to unit. On one unit, there was an interesting resident who was on my assignment, but there was no explanation about the resident. While I was on my way to go and see them, I was stopped by another CNA, who told me about an interesting resident: "He's blind, he's sitting in a recliner, he was a boxer and is very nervous, and the worst part, you can't let him know when you are going to put him in bed."

Listen to this: I talk to my residents all the time, telling them what I'm doing, but I could not tell this one. I don't know if he would respond to anything.

My intention was to get his chair close to the bed. I wondered why he was not on the Hoyer Pad.

He wasn't assigned to one.

I don't know how it happened so fast, but within a second, the resident was in bed. I even surprised myself. You should have seen the look on his face. My eyes glanced towards the door; I saw a green light over the bed, and then I heard the nurse asking me if the resident was in bed. She would be the first to write a report on me if anything had happened. I remember on my unit one night, I had this resident ready for bed; most of them went in different ways. This guy was big, over two hundred pounds.

In this unit, only a curtain divided the beds in the rooms. I had to pick him up from the wheelchair and then put him onto the bed. When I was almost finished, the other resident said, "Pam, you put him in already?"

I didn't hear a sound, so how come when other people put him in, I hear so much groaning and all the racket? I said, "Everyone is different."

He said, "You certainly are." This one called me Brown Sugar.

This resident I am talking about was the most sociable of the unit, and you could not take him lightly. He will take pictures with you; one time, I tried to escape, telling him, "I'm busy." The nurse even helped me out, but guess what? He caught up with me on the other side. That resident knew everyone and got along with three-quarters of the workers. You have to feed him; he couldn't do anything for himself. A pointer was tied around his hand so he could touch a button on the elevator; he could ride his chair in there and go to any floor he wished. When you saw the situation these residents were in, you would do everything in your power to help them; the best is good enough for me. I go home and feel I've done my best.

Back then, we tried to make their life bearable. Once there was a happy birthday wishes for me and another coworker, on the intercom from the security at the desk, and there were birthday surprises on our break time (we would catch a little food on the run). I was always at work on my birthday; once, I didn't even know when the day came. So this birthday I probably got it off, and there was a surprise plan for both of us. I remember the size flan her mother made for me the last time. This time, I don't know what was made. Listen to this: one morning at about ten o'clock, I heard someone say, "Pam, you have flowers at the lobby," and then the intercom came on: "Pam, come get your flowers at the lobby."

I looked at the nurse and asked, "What flowers?"

No one knew. I shook my head a little to come back to my senses, and then said, "Why didn't he send them home?"

I said, "Oh boy, what is the date today?" When they told me, I said, "It's my anniversary."

You should have seen the resident's face, saying, "You forgot?"

I said, "He always does it that way, so I could remember the day."

One of my coworkers said, "Pam, you are funny, and you are not making it up; it just happened and came out that way."

I told her, "One of my girls always say, 'Mummy, you are funny.'"

Unfortunately, they removed her from the floor with all that seniority. When I came to work and heard she was not there, I saw a resident. She said, "Pamelita," (that's what she called me), "you look lonely."

I said, "I am lonely, and I feel lonely, because you are not expecting a switch, when we need more workers coming."

That taught me to be independent and rely on what I can do.

One night, I was working with this other CNA, showing him the ropes. I had this resident, over two hundred pounds, line up at the side of the bed and told this other CNA what to do: remove her chair as soon as I picked her up, because I wanted the space to turn her around as fast as I could, but oh no, it didn't happen. That resident slammed me across the bedside table right into the wall and landed on top of me. My knee twisted, my whole body twisted; I had to use every muscle that I had left to push and struggle to get that resident onto the bed, and then I turned around to see if the wall had a hole in it. I thought we both went through it. Then I looked up at the CNA, standing there with the chair in place. I believe I felt better knowing the wall wasn't broken and the resident was safe.

The supervisor was informed quickly (the resident in a room with a phone), so I said to her, "Did you hear what happened?"

She said, "I thought the closet over there had fallen down."

So the supervisor got all the information from her. After a few days, I had to go to therapy for my knee; they took an x-ray, and an MRI was done on my entire body.

I don't know why I didn't get mad with that CNA. I was really super calm, but guess what? He went on with other CNAs, and they didn't take his crap; they told the supervisor on him, and he was gone.

I already mentioned this resident who called me Flash Gordon. I remember on the three-to-eleven shift one Christmas holiday, her husband came to visit her when I was working; this was a person who usually just said, "Hi, how are you?"

That gentleman thanked me from the bottom of his heart, saying how much he appreciated that I spent my holiday taking care of his wife. You would think it was a speech with a medal to follow, because on holidays, people often called in sick or requested it off. After he left, his wife said, "I didn't know he had it in him."

She had never heard him talk like that before. My opinion is that when they come to visit, you don't know how much they observe. No one ever beat this resident in Scrabble; her brain is the sharpest of them all. She is getting weaker; I hope she will be able to read this book.

As the years go by, I didn't listen to the other CNAs, who said that you cannot run to every call light. My response was, they need something. A few years later, I was having a problem with my foot and had to be taken off the floor. I went to a smaller unit that consisted of fewer residents and very little walking. I spent a few months there; while I was there, the residents were trying to find out where I was. So one asked the supervisor, and she was told the supervisor would inform me that they were asking for me.

A couple of days later, the phone rang, and the nurse smiled and said, "It's for you, Pam."

Let me tell you, this resident only uses the phone by the side of her bed; knock it once and the operator comes on. She gives them all the information required and she'll find you. After I was treated, I went back to my floor.

I remember on the second shift, this resident's face was always turned towards the door; if you were a new worker and didn't pay attention, you'd get in trouble. So this worker came to the unit and couldn't find anything to do; two evenings in a row, he went into a room in front of this other resident's door.

She told me, "He's hiding from work; if he keeps it up, I'm going to tell the supervisor he's watching TV."

I said to the worker, "Do you know that resident across the hall is alert? She sees you every time you go in that room, right in front of her."

He asked, "What?"

But after a while, he flew the coop.

When I was making arrangements for my morning shift, a supervisor asked me, "Where do you want to work?"

I froze for a while, and then guess what? I said, "I like my floor, but they are so demanding."

She said, "I am going to float you for a while, because I can't make this decision alone; we supervisors have to come together."

So when I went to this floor, this CNA started packing up her things. I asked, "Why?"

She said, "Because you have more seniority over me."

I said, "Hold up, you aren't going anywhere, because I'm not staying."

I don't know why I said that, but I didn't feel I would be staying. About three weeks later, the office told me that I was going back to my floor. Oh boy! I thought I was going to heaven, my home away from home. When I got back, an assignment was awaiting me; the other CNAs started complaining that I had just come and already got an assignment.

Someone else said, "You just came, what you are talking about? You don't know her from the other shift."

So I had this resident on my assignment; she talked to me and said, "Thank you, Pam, for staying until you got full time."

I made some people happy and some sad; my afternoon residents were the sad ones. When one of them saw me, she started crying.

I said, "People will think I did something to you," but she could not stop crying. She missed me so much on the three-to-eleven shift. I didn't know what to say to her.

This must be a hard choice to make, because CNAs who are now nurses were saying they were sorry they became nurses. The responsibilities are much greater. This chapter of my life, I didn't know I would be writing books after school; my first job with a real paycheck had been a secretary in a law firm and then a real estate agency. But all my life, business was where I grew up. First, I got in housekeeping, working for a lawyer and his wife, a businesswoman. I returned again and worked with one of the largest hotels in housekeeping, until I finally got my CNA license. The first CNA job I got, a resident told me, "You love to work the hard way."

I said to him, "What do you mean?"

He said, "The other girls come in here with a wet wash cloth, but you have a basin of water in your hand."

For him, I did what he asked and continued with my daily task. I couldn't do for everyone the way he thought it should be. He saw them with a wash cloth and was glad; he saw me with a basin and got mad.

One resident I had back in the early years was the only child for his mother. Several times a week, she would come to see him. I said, "Sometimes you can't understand what he is saying."

She smiled and said, "He speaks another language, which is French, so that's what you are hearing."

So time and years went by; my primary assignment changed, but when he would see me, he would remind me of when I used to have him as a primary. A couple of residents would be sitting in the hallway, waiting for their meds; I would pass by, and one would ask me, "What are your secrets?"

I replied, "What secret?" But then it came to mind that I was always faced with challenging residents, and I tried to do the best I can.

When we were kids, my father told us, "Hard work never killed anyone." I never stopped talking about it, because I couldn't figure it out.

I came to my senses two years ago. I told my coworker my father never worked for anyone, he had people working for him. The lady said, "Your father is a smart man."

My brother only laughed when we talked about what he said; he never said he was wrong or right. I had to find out for myself. One thing I know, I found out the hard way:

I can't quit, I won't quit, I'll never quit. When you are in the driver's seat, all you see is the road ahead; you can't turn back or turn around, only continue.

Changing over to the morning shift, my alarm clock was what I depended on, until I no longer needed it. I could get up on a click; after a while, I didn't need the alarm. It was in March, when the time changes; I went to bed early, so I didn't know if anyone changed the clocks. I woke up, confused, and looked at every clock; each one said a different time. I could not wait around for anything; I could not be an hour late. I decided to go outside; it was pitch black. I said, "It's better to be early than an hour late."

Well, on the way to work, I didn't see two cars pass by. I was still thinking, *I hope I'm not late.* When I reached the parking lot, there was not a soul in sight. When I got inside, everyone on the night shift was smiling when they heard the story. I was one hour early. It didn't take much for that hour to pass.

I always told one resident I had on the morning shift that she should cut her hair a little shorter. I began to style her hair for her. She told me that when the other shift came in, they would ask, "Did you go to the beauty parlor today?"

She would say, "No."

They would ask, "Who styled your hair?" and she would say, "Pam." She got a lot of compliments, and then she said, "You didn't know you had it in you."

Another resident I had for a few years told her family I took care of her hair, and her daughter took care of her nails. From time to time, our residents would get switched over to other CNAs. Whenever I would see them in the hallway, if something was not right, I would try and fix it for them.

One resident was interesting; most of the resident were in their forties and fifties; I had the youngest and the oldest. The youngest communicated by writing. The oldest was very alert; she said she was lost without me. She even tried to ask me where I'll be on my days off.

When I changed to the morning shift, another chapter in my life began. When another challenge begins, you cannot waste a minute of it; the clock is ticking. Residents were now putting their demands in; a ninety-nine-year-old resident said, "Get me up as soon as possible when you come in." Another resident wanted to get up at 7:30, and others wanted to sleep in till nine. The breakfast was around the corner, waiting to be served. On top of that, you had to listen to the report in the morning, and you had to feed them, set up the trays, clear them, and get the food trucks back in place. You had to have some understanding workers and pray everything works out fine, or else your whole world could turn upside down. To top it off, all these residents were alert; it was the MS unit, which consisted of over forty residents.

A resident once said, "You have a lot of patience with people."

"Why?" I asked.

"Because you were in here and then I heard you talk to a resident outside."

I said, "She was sitting at the door and the call light was on. I know her primary was nowhere near this side on the unit, so I helped her out a little, and then I told her to put the call light on; a nurse will pass by and answer it."

My door was in front of her door, so I could see and hear anything happening over that side. It happened to someone who appreciated what you do for her. It happened quite a few times, I was taking care of my resident, and they said I was like Mother Theresa.

I asked, "Why?" But I kept on going, so I didn't hear the answer.

I heard that CNAs were not willing to adopt another CNA's help from residents by telling them how someone gets along by themselves. They don't even try to listen to the residents; the offer was turned down, by saying, "I know how to do my work, don't tell me."

I'm glad to listen because something else may work for you. I've gotten tips from residents; they are not forcing you, it's up to you, because finding someone when you are ready just to pull someone up in bed could cost you a long time coming.

Some people told me they could not work with alert residents; I said, "I prefer them because they will tell the truth, or if they are lying, you will know."

One girl told me, "Give me the crazy one's fighting or running away. I'll do my job, but not with alert people; that's my choice." When she came to the alert unit, she looked so confused.

Back where I started with the MS residents, I was seeing different residents and new equipment and different approaches on people that I never saw before. Every day, you would hear something different about how the residents were, but then when it's your turn, you have to be really cautious and play it safe, but on the other hand, you have to be more alert and not get confused by them. I learned about motorized chairs and then computerized chairs. I tried for a couple of days and didn't get it, but one final day I said, "Heck with it." I turned that thing on and made up my mind what will be will be; the chair was in motion and everything was in order, tilting, backing up, turning around. I amazed myself.

I heard the resident say, "When you are good, you are good."

I had that chair like a baby now. You can do anything you really want; it's all about you.

Another chapter in my life; I cannot forget this one. One morning, a coworker and I were putting a resident in her chair, when the other worker noticed that the Hoyer lift was not stopping. The residents heard this and start screaming. I had to move quickly from my position and come to the front; I released the pad as fast as possible. Now the arms of the Hoyer lift were resting on the chair; the resident was feeling the pressure and crying like crazy. The buttons were turned off, and the other helper told me to go get help.

I said, "No time to panic."

I was doing everything in my power to take the Hoyer off the resident. The lift finally came off; it never stopped at any time. When it came to the end, only a baby could crawl under it. I stood there in amazement, just looking, as the resident thanked us for saving her life.

At the time of panic, you have to be calm, so your brain can take over. When she told the other workers about it, she said, "Pam was super cool." For me, in all the years, I had never seen anything like that happen. It was the biggest and most dangerous struggle; I was afraid what would happen to the resident, but God was with us all that time. All I could think of was *This cannot happen*; you would have to see it to believe it. She was never bruised or pressured hard in any way. She said, "Pam, I thank you for saving my life."

There was another MS resident; workers were afraid of her, I don't know why, because I got along with her, she was the one that kept us in her room until supper was over that day, it must have been a test, there was always a smile on her face when she saw me. She always tried to be pleasant; one day, she asked, "Who gave you your name?"

I told her, "A teacher gave it to my mother."

She said, "It's a pretty name." I was curious myself, so I asked my mother; that's how I knew how I got my name. Another resident, who was ninety years old, said I had a pretty name. She was deaf and wore two hearing aids. Sometimes I would say something, not expecting an answer, and she answered me.

One of my residents who admired everything said, "You make the workplace cheerful." Sometimes, something you say to them just makes their day.

This resident was very observant; she said to the other CNAs that I was the best in helping the other CNAs.

45

This one takes me back only a few weeks ago. Floaters were on the floor: CNAs who did not have much seniority. Once in a while, you'd see different people on the unit. So this frightened me as people were sitting down to sign their books. One CNA asked someone, "Do you help people?"

The girl looked up; I looked up, and she asked, "Why don't you help other people?"

The other girl asked, "Are you talking to me?"

I recognized two different accents. The conversation wasn't getting any prettier. Then she looked across and told me, "You are the only one they ever talk about how you help everybody. People on every floor talk about you."

One thing I can say, people never hesitated to ask me for help, and I don't know how anyone could work in this field without help.

When I was on my other shift, workers often asked me, "Why are your residents so nice?"

"Because you are nice," she said. "You treat them nice."

I had a resident who was harder to break, but they were slowly showing kindness. I was off for one day, and our nurse told me she caught hell. She said, "Pam, I passed through hell the day you weren't here."

I said, "I believe you."

The night nurse laughed; most of the time, we lost our break time still doing residents, but for me, I didn't care that much. I would rather see the residents out of bed for their lunch breaks.

In the meantime, I'm *Dodging Food*, which is the title of my next book. I thank everyone who crossed my path, because I could not do it alone. Thank you all from the bottom of my heart.

www.ingramcontent.com/pod-product-compliance
Lightning Source LLC
Chambersburg PA
CBHW030540290526
45786CB00004B/1801